A
FRIEND
Makes
All The
DIFFERENCE

by Jane Parker Resnick

The C. R. Gibson Company,
Norwalk, Connecticut
06856

To _Martha Lynn_

At first I thought, this is silly, giving you a book to say the things I really want to say myself. But then I knew I would never find the words. The thoughts expressed here are so like my own. Here then is a token of my friendship, a reminder that I'm very glad you're my friend.

Happy Birthday,

Bobbye

Illustrations by Betsy Beach
Designed by Carleen Carreras
Editorial direction by Jayne Bowman
Set in Zapf International Italic

HEARTFELT emotions have a way of staying in the heart. Even the simplest seem too hard to say out loud. And the message is simple. For all of the reasons you found here, I'm so glad you are my friend. I think you know that. And as the pace of our lives continues, punctuated by events, planned or unpredictable, our lives will be enhanced by our friendship in ways that only we can make possible. And that is something to look forward to.

Thank you for being my friend.

THE future is something we sometimes talk about but even the firmest of plans are merely sketches of what tomorrow may bring. Only time can fill in the details. Yet I feel sure of some things. Even if we were to be separated by distance or preoccupied by life's most pressing tasks, we would still be friends. Neither the interruption of miles nor the passing of time could change the good feeling between us. Friends, close as you and I, don't become distant just because they are apart.

"*FAMILY*" *is a word reserved for the people* born *to be closest to you. They have a birthright to the title which is simply automatic. But brothers and sisters, cousins and uncles and aunts aside, it seems to me that we have* become *"family" to one another. We are related because we want to be, not because we happen to be. And a family feeling between friends is some-thing to cherish. It shows a depth of caring beyond the ordinary.*

*F*RIENDSHIP *is a connecting line between two people, at times a lifeline, at times the most delicate of threads. The bond depends on each side holding fast to its end. Well, I'm not letting go of my side and it's a wonderful feeling to know that yours is anchored just as well. It's great to know that with a tug or a pull from either side we can call upon each other. There'll always be someone at the other end.*

BEING your friend has some benefits that are purely personal. Knowing that you value my friendship is something I really take pride in. Seeing that you trust my opinion gives me the courage to voice it elsewhere. Including me in your life has shown me how to include others in mine. With you I have gained not only friendship, but possibilities.

*T*HERE are some ways that I have benefited from our friendship that you may not even realize. Because of you, I am more accepting of myself. If you see good qualities in me, then they must be there. If you perceive capabilities, then I know I can somehow put them to use. And if I try and fail, I know I can still depend on your encouragement. What I have gained, you have offered instinctively, unaware of the difference in me there would be without you.

*I*F I had to look at the world without your eyes, my vision would be so much poorer. Your point of view means a lot to me. It broadens my focus and sharpens the images of what I see. It gives me perspective and that makes all the difference.

When I share my thoughts with you, they take a new, informed shape. As I share my dreams with you, they become possibilities. You are a mirror for me in which I see myself more clearly.

CHOICES and decisions are life's puzzles and I often turn to you for answers when there really are no answers, just alternatives. But your suggestions help me weigh the pros and cons and your insight helps me clarify my thoughts. The decision might be difficult and my final choice, even if made alone, might have been the same. But your willingness to listen and well-intentioned help give me such relief and comfort. I really feel as if I'm not choosing alone.

LET's dream. I'm planning a vacation and I want you to come. We'll forget all our responsibilities. (Now there's a dream!) We'll leave obligations behind. Tear up schedules. Make tracks for fresh air and sunshine. Or immerse ourselves in cityscape—restaurants and fancy shops. Hours will blend with ease into days that fly by in the company of a good friend. Share my dream. It may be just a fantasy but it sure is fun.

*W*HATEVER *I'm doing, I find myself stor-
ing up images to share with you later. I uncon-
sciously collect impressions to bring to our
conversations. I keep a mental journal of
recollections, details and descriptions to draw
on when we are together. It's great fun to recreate
my experiences for you and even more fun to see
your reactions.*

*T*HERE *are some activities that I enjoy but
you do not and other things that you like to do
that I would rather not. But when we get
together and talk about our experiences, the
pleasure somehow increases. It's fun, I think,
because we accept each other's interests and
appreciate what they mean to each of us. It
pleases us both to give each other a chance to
share our separate pleasures.*

DID you ever notice how much we talk? Talk on the phone. Talk while we're eating. Or riding in the car. Or doing our shopping. Or while we should be working. It may sound like talk about nothing but it's really talk about everything. We think out loud, exchange experiences and ask questions about ourselves and others. No matter that answers are elusive or decisions inconclusive, we share insights and approaches and feel relief that our thoughts have been aired. And finally, we know that the moment's discussion will, inevitably, be the subject of more talk.

*W*OULDN'T it be marvelous if we had the luxury of more time together. We could free ourselves from the press of moment-to-moment obligations and nourish our spirits with leisurely conversation. We could laugh long and hard at old jokes remembered and new ones discovered. But time is hard to find and the brevity of ours together makes it all the more valuable. So when we do have the time, we must make it count. Enjoy the conversation and treasure the laughter. Time passes but the laughter lasts.

I don't think we're ever bored when we're together. We make each other laugh, although others may find the humor missing. We make each other see things in different ways, although we're both reluctant to revise our points of view. Having each other along, we bring ourselves wholeheartedly—and that is never boring.

*S*OMETIMES I think we have the best time revising history, just talking about what has already happened, bending events with our peculiar sense of humor, warping them to fit our point of view. Take a sad event and before our talk is through we will put that sorrow in its proper place. Our pasts would just be moments gone by if we didn't have each other to make them last.

It's clear that our friendship is no guarantee that we will never disagree. Our opinions in some matters will always be opposed. Regardless of convincing arguments and good reasons, some ideas are carved in stone and some feelings too deeply rooted to be swayed. So we expect that in some areas what I see as black, you will see as white, and there will be no gray. And, even though it's hard at times, we accept the difference.

I used to think that friendship only meant going places together, making dates and having plans, but I was missing the point. It's great when we can do these things together, but our friendship isn't based on social occasions. At times, we have no chance to see each other. The phone is our gathering place and heartfelt conversation is our occasion. Even though we're apart, we're together, talking about real concerns and daily trivialities, commiserating over problems and celebrating successes. We don't only share events, we share our lives.

*A*s a friend, you make it possible for me to be a friend. You allow me to help you when you need help. You depend on me when you need to recount the day's woes, or think out loud, or toast a small victory. You count on me to calm your fears and encourage your ambitions. And you turn to me with good news because to me your triumphs are cause for celebration. In this way, I can be a person who listens and cares, who gives comfort and shares delight. And that's good. I'm a better person for it—and a better friend.

I have always found it difficult to ask other people to do things for me. This is hardly a virtue, but a certain shyness and reluctance to impose. I'd rather try to be in two places at the same time than ask anyone to be there for me. Except you. It is a measure of my belief in our friendship that I feel perfectly comfortable asking for your help at any time. If I express my need, I know you will respond and I, of course, would do the same for you. It's not a matter of requests and favors but a simple desire to help each other out. And that makes asking easy.

SINCE we've been friends, I know that someone will remember my birthday—and call it young. Send me funny postcards—when I wish I were there. Listen to my complaints—justified or not. Tolerate my singing—even though that's hard. Take my side—when the side needs taking. Lie a little—when the truth hurts too much. And tell me the truth—if the truth must be known.

And since we've been friends, you have someone who will do that, too.

LET'S face it, vanity counts. When I change my hairstyle or my make-up, or take a few pounds off, or wear a new (and too expensive) dress, I'm really disappointed if all my efforts go unheeded. But I can depend on you to observe even the little things—and to tell me when they need fixing, too. It's the fact that you pay attention that I appreciate. Because you notice, I know you care.

IT is so much fun for me to surprise you with a little present. It's not large, of course, just a small extravagance, an unexpected treat. Seeing that startled look of delight on your face, I feel, for once, that I am giving a little for all that I have received.

THE way I see it, we operate on the same wavelength. Let me explain. It's been my experience that words can only take you so far. You can tell some people one thing, and they will hear another. Others will understand your words, but miss the meaning. But with you, I never have to explain. You always know what I am talking about.

If I give you the facts, you will see the same implications that I do. I don't have to tell you why I think something is marvelous or cruel or ridiculous—you'll know. Sometimes, only a single word is necessary. Or no word at all. A look, a shrug, a smile, or a grimace is enough to communicate a whole range of meanings between us. The message isn't telepathic, but it isn't tangible either. It's something mutual and exclusive, flashing from my mind to yours across a wavelength of understanding.

*H*OW many people feel they have a friend who understands the twists of their emotions, the personal bent of their motivations? How many people have a friend who can say, "I know what that means to you," and actually do know?

Most people think no one really understands them and that may be true. But you understand me, all right, and probably better than I do myself. Once in awhile you even let me get away with more than a pretense or two, if you think it's necessary, to soften a disappointment, or bolster my confidence, or help me over the rough edges of life's jagged moments. This understanding is more than kindness, it is a clear vision of the person that is me.

*F*RIENDSHIP is supposed to be a matter of give and take and so I want to thank you for all the times I "took" and maybe took for granted. I've leaned on your sympathy, I've imposed on your good nature, and I've strenuously bent your ear. It seems to me that I have taken more than my share and you have given more than yours.

I've taken your thoughtful advice, discarded it, and willfully fallen right on my face. I've taken your time to vent my frustration, voice my complaints and worry out loud. And I can hear you say, "But that's what friends are for." And I can only say that I am truly blessed.

WITH most people I have trouble letting my guard down. It's as if a small part of me issues protective orders: "Don't say the wrong thing." "Don't appear unsure." "Don't admit to weakness." I'm not quite certain what there is to fear, but still the barrier stays up and I remain behind.

But with you, there are no walls. It's possible that the chemistry of real friendship was just right for us and the barrier never existed, but I don't believe so. I think you gently pushed the barricade aside, and seeing my fear, made me feel secure and let me be myself. I know I didn't do it alone. I couldn't have even though I would have wanted to.

THIS book is a jubilation. A red-letter day in your honor. Trumpets and fanfare, please! A drumroll! A triumphant, loud ovation! These pages are a celebration, a toast, a salute to you, my friend—for being my friend.

This is the moment to sum up, to take stock, to tell you what your friendship means to me. Because of you there is more joy and laughter and compassion and honesty in my life. Now is the time for you to enjoy the pleasure you bring to me.